Children
at War

Bridget Daly and
Jenny Vaughan

Macdonald

A MACDONALD BOOK

© Donna Bailey Ltd 1988

First published in Great Britain in 1988 by
Macdonald & Co. (Publishers) Ltd
London and Sydney
A BPCC plc company

ISBN 0 356 13738 4

Editor Donna Bailey
Production Controller Julia Mather
Picture Research Elizabeth Loving
Designed by Jim Weaver

Printed in Portugal by
Printer Portuguesa

Macdonald & Co. (Publishers) Ltd
Greater London House
Hampstead Road
London NW1 7QX

BRITISH LIBRARY
CATALOGUING IN PUBLICATION DATA
Daly, Bridget
   Children at war. – (Children in Conflict)
   1. Children and war
   I. Title   II. Vaughan, Jennifer
   305.2′3   HQ784.W3   III. Series
   ISBN 0-356-13738-4

Credits

The publishers would like to thank the following for
   use of their copyright material:

Andes Press Agency: 34 (Jon Bennett), 36 (Julian
   Filochowski), 39b
Aldus Archive: 9t, 16, 29b
Associated Press: 31t
BBC Hulton Picture Library: 32–33t
Camera Press: 8, 9b, 14, 21r, 27b, 28, 30, 35b, 37b
Daisy Hayes: 20–1
Keystone: 32–3b
Rashid Lombard: 6b
Mansell Collection: 10, 11t
© 1977 Marvel Comics UK: 19
Popperfoto: 5, 15. 18r, 22, 24, 25 both, 35t, 39t, 41b
Punch Magazine: 11b
Rex: cover both, 4, 6t, 7, 12, 13 both, 17 both, 18l,
   20l, 23 both, 26, 27t, 29t, 33r, 37t, 40, 41t
Chris Steele-Perkins/Save The Children Fund: 31b
Mike Wells: 38

Contents

What is war?

1986 was named the United Nations Year of Peace. But by the end of the year 36 wars and conflicts were taking place, involving some 5 million fighters from over 40 nations. What, then, makes wars start?

Firstly, wars do not just suddenly start out of the blue. They are the result of long-standing arguments between one nation and another, or between communities within the same nation. The normal way of solving these disputes is by 'diplomacy', which means that the leaders meet, talk and bargain. It is only when these talks break down and one or both sides decide to take what they want by force, that wars begin.

There are many reasons why wars are fought. They may be fought over boundaries, where both sides want the same piece of land because their own is overcrowded or poor. They may be fought over material possessions, such as valuable minerals like gold. The rulers of one country may have a

Below Friend or foe? This little girl looking anxiously over her shoulder is an innocent victim of a war which has been going on for 60 years in a mountainous region of Asia called Kurdestan. She has lived all her short life in the shadow of fear and insecurity, as her village is under constant threat of air attack. Women and children must act as look-outs, as many of the men have either been killed, imprisoned or are hiding out in the hills.

Above This is no game. These young Mozambicans were part of an adult army, learning to use real guns and rocket launchers in their war of independence. They were young – but probably considered themselves quite old enough to fight. International law states that children should not bear arms until they are 15 years old, but this is often hard to impose. Some children are recruited into armies because they are needed to add to the numbers of troops. Others, like these teenagers, want to fight, and adults do not stop them. They may want to avenge friends and relatives they have seen die, and to play a part in the struggle for freedom and their own future security.

particular religion or a political system that they believe in so strongly that they think the rest of the world should adopt it. Or one country may feel threatened by its neighbour, so its leaders may try to create a civil war within the neighbouring country. They may sell arms to an opposition group who want to take power, and encourage this group to cause unrest. Or the native people of a country occupied by a colonial power may start a war to gain their independence.

It is usually the leaders of a country or a community who decide to start fighting. Most ordinary people hate war, so they have to be persuaded that a war is right and necessary. This is quite easy if the reason for the war is obvious. Perhaps one group is much richer than the other. But often people have to be educated to believe that the other group or nation is more stupid, cruel, less civilized and more aggressive than their own. This then makes it much easier to justify making war against them.

Undeclared wars

Many conflicts throughout the world are not officially called 'wars'. That is to say, they do not start with a breakdown of discussions by leaders or politicians around a conference table. They grow up gradually, starting perhaps with people's protests, followed by riots on the streets. The army might then be brought in to help the police keep control. Then the rioters get guns and make their own petrol bombs, the army starts shooting, and a civil conflict has begun. This kind of fighting usually takes place between different communities within one country, but sometimes other countries are asked to come in to help one side or another. If this happens, there is a danger that the situation will turn into a full-scale war between the two nations involved.

When protests and riots do not get the results that people want, they may organize themselves into secret, civilian armed groups. When they then fight the government forces, this is known as 'guerrilla' warfare. 'Guerrilla' means 'little

Above Children born at the beginning of the present 'troubles' in Northern Ireland are now nearly 20 years old. Those living in the centre of Belfast have grown up with the familiar sight of armed British troops and the sound of armoured cars rumbling through the streets. The baby in the pram may have heard gunfire many times before. The soldier is prepared to shoot at any moment – and there is a chance that the pram could be caught in the cross-fire.

Above A petrol-bombed car blazes behind him as a boy cycles down the street. In the townships of South Africa there is no escape from the conflict, which has been called 'the war against the children'. Thousands of young black people have been killed, wounded, imprisoned and tortured because of their opposition to the racist system of *apartheid* under which their country is governed. What started as peaceful demonstrations in the mid-1970s against second-rate education for blacks, has been followed by major riots and petrol-bombing. The security forces have attacked people with guns and dogs, and have shown no mercy – arresting children as young as eight years old.

war' after the Spanish word for war *guerra*. The guerrilla fighters go on living in their own towns and villages, but mount sudden, surprise attacks on government troops. It is very difficult to catch guerrillas, as once they have made an attack, they vanish into their towns and villages again, and no one knows their identity.

Children are particularly at risk in civil conflicts and guerrilla wars. They may have fathers or brothers in the guerrilla force who get killed in action or are taken away by the government troops. Villages are often raided by troops searching for the guerrillas, and women and children may be killed, wounded or taken prisoner along with the men. Families may have to leave their homes because their houses have been burned or bombed.

Children are often involved in the fighting in these conflicts. They grow up believing in the cause that their father or older brother is fighting for, even though they may not really understand it. They are forced to grow up very quickly. With fighting all around them, it is not surprising that they want to take their place beside the older members of their family in the struggle. So, even as young as seven or eight years old, they act as spies or messengers, man barricades or throw bricks and petrol bombs.

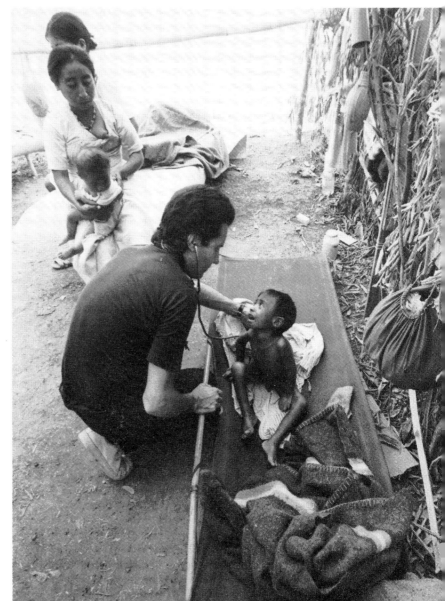

Right A French doctor in Honduras treats a small refugee boy from El Salvador who has been so disturbed by the horrors that he witnessed at home that he could not eat, drink or talk. Civil war has been going on for several years. In 1980 government troops decided to clear civilians out of an area near the Honduran border. But instead of evacuating the civilians, they bombed the villages and drove the people out. The little boy ran as fast as he could and swam across to the other side of the Sanpul river. He watched in horror as his family – who did not escape in time – were brutally tortured and killed.

Never again

The Holocaust is the name given to the near destruction of the Jewish race in Europe by the German Nazis during World War II. It was a unique historical event, both in its horror and its scope. Six million men, women and children were put to death in a planned extermination programme, just because they were born Jews. How could this terrible thing have happened?

After World War I, Germany was in chaos. There was soaring inflation, the economy was static and millions became unemployed. There was no welfare state, so people literally starved. Discontent spread.

In 1933, the National Socialists (Nazis) came to power under their leader Adolf Hitler. Their popularity had grown very quickly because they had a strong, simple message: a dictatorship would end political chaos, nationalism would lead to the expansion of Germany and wealth for all. Lastly the Nazis needed to channel the people's discontent by blaming someone else for the country's problems. They picked on the Jews.

Hitler did not invent racism against the Jews. That had been in existence for

Above Jewish children, desperate with hunger, slip through the walls of the Warsaw ghetto in Poland, risking their lives for a morsel of food. The Nazis concentrated the Jews in Germany and Poland into ghettos in the cities. To boost German industry and the war effort, labour camps were set up for all Jews aged 14 to 60. They were forced to work 12 to 16 hours a day. Inside the ghetto, behind the barbed wire, the Jews lived, overcrowded, unfed, unpaid and unclothed. Many died, especially children, from hunger, cold, disease and beatings. Survivors were sent to the concentration camps.

hundreds of years. He just used it, claiming that the Jews were an inferior race and that they had become too powerful and wealthy, and were taking away jobs and money from the Germans. He used lies, propaganda and vicious cartoons to turn the people against the Jews.

Gradually all rights were taken away from Jews. By 1938 they were excluded from every area of public life. They were herded into ghettos and employed as slave labour. By 1940 much of Europe was under German control and millions of Jewish people with it. In 1942 the Final Solution was implemented which legally allowed the Jews to be exterminated.

Above On January 20 1942, a conference of top Nazi officials listed fourteen million Jews throughout occupied Europe who were to be annihilated. Promises were made to the Jews of 'resettlement', better conditions, food and work. At first voluntarily, and later by force, millions were herded into sealed cattle trucks which carried them across the railways of Europe in dark, filthy conditions to the death camps. Over 1,000 people might be transported this way in one day to a single camp.

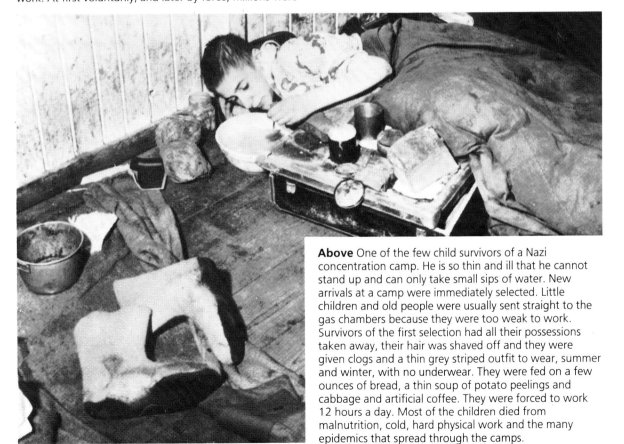

Above One of the few child survivors of a Nazi concentration camp. He is so thin and ill that he cannot stand up and can only take small sips of water. New arrivals at a camp were immediately selected. Little children and old people were usually sent straight to the gas chambers because they were too weak to work. Survivors of the first selection had all their possessions taken away, their hair was shaved off and they were given clogs and a thin grey striped outfit to wear, summer and winter, with no underwear. They were fed on a few ounces of bread, a thin soup of potato peelings and cabbage and artificial coffee. They were forced to work 12 hours a day. Most of the children died from malnutrition, cold, hard physical work and the many epidemics that spread through the camps.

Powder monkeys and drummer boys

Children have been part of armies and navies throughout history. In primitive societies, children were involved in fighting when the survival of the tribe was at stake. In some parts of the world, boys took part in warfare as part of a traditional initiation into manhood. It was not until 1977 that an international law was passed forbidding children under the age of fifteen to bear arms. But children are today still actively engaged in fighting wars.

The earliest record of children joining an adult war in large numbers was the tragic Children's Crusade of 1212. Two armies of boys and girls from France and Germany set out, fired with religious zeal, to join Christian soldiers fighting to capture the Holy Land (the area now called Israel) from the Moslems. Many were less than twelve years old. Most never reached the Holy Land. Some died on the way from hunger, cold or illness, others were drowned at sea, or sold as slaves.

Many children in armies were the sons or orphans of soldiers. One Finnish regiment in the seventeenth century had 302 boys registered from the age of one to eighteen! The army generally took good care of the children until they became grown-up soldiers.

Left Warships during the Napoleonic Wars often had so many young boys aboard that they used to be called the 'nursery ships'. Boys throughout history have been drawn by the lure of the sea. They could join up at the age of ten or eleven as officers' servants and they learnt every aspect of shipboard life, often graduating to ship's master at the age of twenty or twenty-one, with already ten years of service behind them. In wartime they were often employed, like the boy in the picture, as 'powder monkeys', carrying paper cartridges of gunpowder in leather carrying cases from the ship's powder store to the cannons.

Frederick the Great of Prussia in the eighteenth century said: 'Come children, die with me for the Fatherland'. He meant 'children' literally, because many of his soldiers were boys in their teens, the sons of poor noblemen. Their army careers had started at the age of eight.

The situation changed in Europe in the nineteenth century, when conscription armies were brought in and there was less need for uniformed children. It was not until just before World War I that children were again used in a wartime situation, with the foundation of various paramilitary organizations for boys. They were used in World Wars I and II behind the lines in office work, aeroplane observation and as orderlies.

Left Most boys in European armies, before conscription was brought in in the nineteenth century, were the sons or orphans of soldiers. They were usually used as musicians in regimental bands, or as tailors and shoe-menders. These Russian boys were captured by the British in the Crimean War of 1854-6. It was a very hard life in the Crimea for these boy soldiers. They lived in cold, draughty tents, and conditions were so insanitary that many more people died from illness than were killed in the actual fighting.

Right The British government launched a huge propaganda campaign at the start of World War I to encourage men to join the armed forces. Leaflets, newspaper articles and posters urged people to fight for the glory of King and country against the menace of the 'Hun'. It was not surprising that, carried away by the war fever that swept the country, young boys of thirteen and fourteen lied about their age in order to be allowed to join up. When hundreds of mothers protested and questions were asked in Parliament, under-age boys were weeded out and sent home again.

Officer (to boy of thirteen who, in his effort to get taken on as a bugler, has given his age as sixteen). "DO YOU KNOW WHERE BOYS GO WHO TELL LIES?"
Applicant. "TO THE FRONT, SIR."

In the firing line

'Children who have not attained the age of fifteen years shall neither be recruited into the armed forces nor allowed to take part in the hostilities' (Geneva Protocol II, 1977). So runs international law. It seems clear enough: after all, we might ask, who *could* believe it right to draft children into an army?

But in wartime, things are not that simple. Far from having to protect children from being made to fight, it is often quite hard to stop them. Children in South Africa, for example, have taken up arms in the form of stones and petrol bombs, and fought bitter battles against the authorities. They believe they have a cause worth fighting for.

Children in the Ugandan civil war of the 1980s fought alongside adult soldiers of the National Resistance Army, which took over the country in 1986. The children played an important part in their victory. Everyone agreed that they had been fine and willing soldiers.

This should not really be surprising. In most countries, children are taught that it is right to fight for what you believe in. The Ugandan children had an extra reason to take up arms. Many had seen their parents murdered, and they wanted to avenge them.

In Iran, religious leaders encourage boys as young as twelve to join the war against Iraq. Those over thirteen may be forced to join the army. These children are often used to search battle areas for mines. They believe that if they die (which is very likely) they will go straight to heaven. After their death, their families get a 'martyr's card' which allows them to buy food more cheaply in supermarkets. In a poor country, this sort of reward can be very tempting.

There seems no doubt that children make good soldiers, and that they often want to fight. The question is, should they be allowed to? Is it right for the very young to be given the power to kill, perhaps without fully understanding what they are doing?

Below Young Palestinian soldiers in Lebanon in 1981. They have been taught to carry arms and have learned to believe that they are fighting a people's war. Their leaders do not see themselves as exploiting children. They are convinced that they are doing the right thing. In countries that are not at war, few people would think it acceptable for children to carry weapons. When there is fighting all around, children are naturally affected. They learn what the war is about, and feel the need to join in.

Above Although most young soldiers are boys, this is not always the case. There are many regular armies that have women and girls in their ranks. Guerrilla armies may include very young girls, along with boys of the same age.

Like their brothers, these Palestinian girls believe they should fight for their people. They are willing to train for battle and to learn to handle weapons, just like the boys.

Left These young Kampucheans were recruited into the armed forces at the age of about twelve. They were usually orphans from very poor families: some were homeless and most were virtually uneducated. The army gave them a home and, in return, they became very disciplined young soldiers, intensely loyal to their leaders. One problem with child soldiers is that they are very intolerant. These young people were often put in charge of prisoners and showed themselves to be extremely ruthless and cruel.

Behind the lines

Children often take part in wars without ever carrying weapons. With so many adults away fighting, they are forced to take over their jobs. During World War II, for example, young children in Britain helped out on the land, growing food for their families and communities. They also helped out by collecting scrap metal for recycling. Shortages are inevitable in wartime, so all this was vital.

In civil wars, children often find themselves doing much more. They may take on a variety of tasks: cooking food for guerrilla soldiers, tending the wounded, or taking over responsibility for whole farms.

They may also become spies, picking up scraps of news about government plans and reporting them to guerrilla movements. This was common in the Zimbabwean war of independence, which went on for most of the

Above This frightened little boy has been caught up in a war he cannot possibly understand. He is a refugee in South Africa at the turn of the century, when the Dutch-speaking Boer farmers fought for independence from the British. On the Boer side whole communities were involved, and children little older than this one acted as spies and messengers in support of their parents' war.

1970s. Children were able to listen in to conversations between adults and among soldiers and learn what their plans were. They were able to pass on messages to the guerrillas who were hiding in the countryside. These children were known as *mujibas*.

Although they did not fight, the mujibas were very powerful. They could save lives by warning people of danger, but they could also point out traitors, who might then be killed. There is no doubt that they helped in winning independence for their country. But after the war was over, some suffered terrible feelings of guilt.

When children take part in a war, they are inevitably treated as enemies by the people they are fighting. In South Africa, for example, where black children have become involved in street fighting in the townships where they live, the authorities have been ruthless. Hundreds of children – some as young as eight years old – have been arrested for offences such as 'intimidation' Many have been injured in prison and will carry the physical and emotional scars for the rest of their lives.

Right Children pull at the heart-strings – and that makes them useful. This picture was taken at the beginning of World War II. It aimed to show the American public how British children were in danger and to persuade the American government to give the British more support. Children were also used in another way: as 'plane spotters', giving advance warning of an enemy air attack. It was exciting work, and the children enjoyed it.

Education or indoctrination?

Education should teach people to think, to ask questions and to see different points of view. There are many ways in which we learn. We are taught at school, we learn from our parents, we read books and newspapers, we watch films, plays and television. In many countries there is relative freedom in media reporting, so people are able to hear many different opinions.

In countries where there is a dictatorship or a totalitarian regime, education and the media are strictly controlled. There people can only learn what the leaders want them to know. This form of education is called 'indoctrication'.

Even in countries which are usually democratic, indoctrination can occur at certain times. During a war, when all political parties agree on the need to go to war, there are often major advertising campaigns with persuasive slogans, which are designed to encourage citizens to support the war effort. This kind of campaign is called 'propaganda'.

Education for war differs widely throughout the world. In some countries, military instruction is a compulsory part of the school system. This includes not only weapon training, drills and fitness classes,

Below Little girls give the Nazi salute at a rally in Hitler's Germany in the 1930s. They look happy enough, but they had no choice but to join in this parade and would have been severely punished if they had not done so. Young people were a particular target for Nazi indoctrination. It was hoped that if the children were caught young enough, they would grow up to become unquestioning, loyal Nazis. Boys were made members of military groups from the age of six. They were given a uniform and started on military drills. Girls were forced into the *Jungmaedel* (Young Maidens) and the *Bund Deutscher Madchen* (League of German Girls). They were taught physical education to prepare them for being healthy mothers when they grew up.

but also lessons in history and politics which inspire patriotism and convince the children that all other nations are inferior to their own.

In countries where there is no specific education for war, ideas of nationalism are still introduced, but in a more subtle way. History lessons usually concentrate on battles that the nation has won, and the lives and deeds of great military leaders. Little or nothing is stated about the numbers of casualties, or whether the reasons for going to war were justified. War is seen as an inevitable and even positive aspect of international affairs.

Left A small boy in the Lebanon volunteers to join the Palestinian cause. He is carried away by the enthusiasm of those who have persuaded him to fight for his people. The Palestinians have been at war with the Israelis for 40 years. Palestinian and Israeli children are both taught a view of their history which encourages them to believe the other side is their enemy, and that their own cause is the only right one. This little boy will probably never be able to judge the situation from anything but his own community's viewpoint.

Right These boys at a religious academy in Iran learn martial arts, judo and karate, by command of Iran's ruler and religious leader, Ayatollah Khomeini. He believes that all children should be brought up to be good Moslems, and he has used his fundamentalist interpretation of Islam as the way to persuade his people to go to war with Iraq. During the current war, all school textbooks have been changed to emphasize the lives of the martyrs, the importance of war and the defence of Islam. In morning assembly, the national anthem has been replaced by hymns wishing long life to Khomeini and death to his enemies. These boys believe that it is their religious duty to fight and die for their country.

The war myth

Throughout history, wars have produced men who have been praised as great military leaders, fearless fighters, or honourable conquerors, such as Alexander the Great, Richard the Lionheart or Napoleon. Their lives are described as full of adventure, excitement and glory. Men followed them without question, and wished to be like them in word and deed.

In the days before stories were written down, people enjoyed listening to travelling story-tellers who told tales of wars fought by bold heroes against incredible odds and fearsome enemies. Nowadays, space heroes hurtle across the universe, overcoming terrifying monsters in order to conquer new worlds. In the old days people listened and imagined the scenes; now we watch them on television or video.

Below If we look at this innocent picture of a small boy being taught the real way to shoulder a gun, we probably see nothing more than a child playing at soldiers. He has seen soldiers like his friend striding along in military parades, the sun glinting on the shiny gold buttons of their dress uniforms, marching to the stirring music of the military brass band. He sees them as heroes and would like to be a soldier when he grows up. But he is a little English boy in the 1980s. He has never seen soldiers struggling back from a war, with half their number dead, and the rest limping on crutches, their eyes glazed and their ordinary khaki uniforms dirty and torn.

But who are these mighty heroes who fire our imaginations and take our thoughts away from the boredom or hardship of everyday life? 'Hero' is a Greek word which meant a man of superhuman strength, courage and ability, one who was favoured by the gods. It later came to mean an illustrious warrior. Whatever the definition, a hero is usually 'good', although this depends which side you are on. It also means that he is selfless enough to die or kill for a country or a belief. (War heroes, apart from women like Joan of Arc or Boadicea, are usually male.)

Above Is there anything so very different about this picture? It is just another sweet, small boy dressed in a uniform, standing proudly next to his hero. It only becomes more sinister when we realize that his hero is Adolf Hitler, who sent millions of other children to their death in the gas chambers because they did not belong to his idea of a pure 'Aryan' race. This picture was used as propaganda during World War II to encourage Germans to support the war effort.

The most important thing about heroes is that they inevitably have myths created around their personalities and actions. These myths usually involve wondrous acts of bravery that our heroes did not, in fact, carry out. The more myths there are, the more they inspire loyalty and make people blindly follow their heroic leaders. The myths always show up their good points, never their bad ones.

Fighting against our hero and his army are the enemy. In literature, and in particular children's literature, the enemy is always cruel, greedy, uncivilized or dangerous, or, at the very least, misguided. These attributes make it seem necessary for our hero either to defend his country against them, or to wipe them out before they become too powerful. It is much harder to come to terms with killing good people.

Right Children love to read comic books, and often these are the only books they read outside school. There are many war comics, which are read almost entirely by boys. Parents often do not discourage children from buying them, because they see it as 'natural' that the boys will read war comics while the girls will read stories of love and romance. War comics are always full of action and adventure, there is never a dull moment. Because they are such an accepted form of reading for boys, they imply that war is as much a part of everyday life as playing football or going to a disco.

War toys

'It's natural, boys will be boys'.
'It's just a phase, they all grow out of it.'
'Well, I had guns when I was a boy, and it never made me go out and kill anyone.'

These are some of the replies that parents give when asked why they buy toy weapons for their little boys. But are their statements true?

Children up to about the age of three tend to be given 'unisex' toys, which are usually brightly-coloured plastic activity toys and the occasional stuffed toy animal. But from then on, toys are usually given according to the child's sex. Girls have dolls or cooking sets, and boys have cars, drills or war toys. Boys are encouraged, and seem to develop on their own, an interest in mechanical things. These either move or have moving parts which the child can exercise control over. The attraction of war toys is that they

Below War toys are a growing industry. In West Germany and France 10 per cent of toy manufacturers make only war toys. The European Parliament is so concerned about war toys that it passed a resolution in 1982. It recognized that war toys give children a liking for weapons, and it recommended that member governments should ban the advertising of war toys, and should ban the manufacture of those that closely resemble real weapons. But, six years later, these children are still able to buy toy uniforms and guns which are made to look just like the real thing.

Above This little Palestinian boy lives in a war zone. He has no money to buy a toy gun – so he has made one, just like the real one his father fights with. He wants to take his place beside his father in the front line, but he is still too young. Pretending is the next best thing. But carrying around toys which closely resemble real weapons, in a war zone, can be very dangerous. From a distance, a trigger-happy soldier might easily mistake the replica for a real gun, and shoot to kill.

very often have all these points: battery-powered tanks and armoured cars have missiles which can be launched, space machines transform into fighting robots, guns have flashing lights, or fire caps, or rubber darts. First, children enjoy making them operate; later they learn that they are for playing fighting and killing games.

Because toys are such big business and provide so many jobs, many governments and toy companies either agree with, or actively encourage the opinion that war toys have nothing to do with real war. Some countries, however, recognize their true function and possibilities.

An official peace delegation from Britain visited the 'under-fives' room of a 'children's palace' in the Soviet Union. In amongst the dolls and stuffed animals was a miniature missile launcher. The staff said that boys must be encouraged to know how to use toy guns and other militaristic equipment, in order to prepare them for their future military obligations.

This followed an announcement from the Soviet Ministry of Retail Trade in 1980: 'Military toys and war games are important from an educational point of view, as they arouse children's interest in, and knowledge of, military techniques, and war games also inspire patriotism.'

So in some ways, the parents' statements are right. If children are never involved in a war and do not have to do military service, then they will probably grow out of their war toys. But what if their country needs to increase its armed forces to go to war? A job which offers the chance to master the technicalities of the large version of the toy machine they played with as a child could seem attractive and exciting to the adult man.

Above You would imagine that the last thing that this boy would want to play with is a war toy. He is a refugee from the Nigerian civil war in Biafra, where thousands of people were killed or made homeless and died of starvation. But he probably finds it difficult to think of anything else but war, so playing with this accurate replica of a rocket, which has somehow found its way into the refugee camp, seems as natural as peacetime children playing with a construction set.

War games

Play is a necessary part of growing up. It is the way we learn the rules of life and how to apply them. Infants play imitative games where they act out situations which they have seen adults involved in. When they are older, they learn to play games with rules which teach them either to co-operate or compete with other players. Competitive games like board games or tennis develop the aggressive side of our personalities. They teach that the aim of the game is to win at all costs. Team games are both competitive and co-operative. We learn how to form alliances with our own team, and to create an imaginary 'enemy' out of the opposing team.

War games are played by children everywhere, in peacetime or war, in pairs or in teams. In countries where children have not known a war, the game is usually no more sophisticated than charging about shouting 'Bang, bang, you're dead!' or ambushing and stalking the enemy. Usually the game ends when one or other side is bored or diverted by something else. It may be that war games during peacetime are, as adults often state, merely harmless fantasy, or a way to work off aggressive energy, but nevertheless, conflict is still seen as something that happens naturally in the adult world, even if it only occurs somewhere far away.

Children in countries which are at war, or children of parents in the armed forces who are stationed in military camps, play very different war games. These children use real strategies, and real military vocabulary. Their games are all about 'attack' and not 'defence'. The games do not end until one side surrenders. The value of the game is greatly increased if the players can get hold of real weapons. The games seem invariably to lead to quarrels. These children seem to see enemies all around them, and think that there is no way of solving problems other than resorting to fighting.

Below It was once said that the Battle of Waterloo was won on the playing fields of Eton. The speaker meant that sports such as this 'field game', played at the famous British public school, encouraged the aggressiveness, team spirit and leadership necessary to win a war. Sports and competitions were first taught to boys in Ancient Greece. They were actually invented to train men for war. Team games were meant to instil a sense of discipline, team co-operation and a desire to win at all costs. Athletics encouraged boys to meet hardships and develop physical endurance.

Above Boys play at war in what was once a symbol of peace and harmony, a religious temple in Kampuchea. These children, living in a strife-torn country with no chance of escape from the fighting, are under a great deal of stress. One of the ways that they try to relieve the stress is to go over and over some of the horrors that they have witnessed in a sort of 'action' replay, by making a game out of them. But in order to be able to carry on a semblance of normal life, after the game is repeated several times, they change the ending. The people are not really dead, only injured, and the children play at taking them to hospital where they will recover.

Right Adults take it for granted that young boys play war games. Boys are encouraged to develop competitiveness and aggression, while girls are taught to be co-operative and gentle. Children who have never been involved in a war cannot fight true-to-life battles. They make up situations based on films or TV programmes, or pretend to be comic book heroes or famous warriors from history.

Luggage and labels

When children are in danger, it usually seems to be a good idea to get them out of it. In World War II, for example, British children were evacuated from the large cities into the countryside, away from the areas being bombed. Some were even sent as far as North America.

Although evacuation probably saved lives, it had its own problems. Children who stayed behind in the cities were frightened when bombs fell, but at least they were with their families. Those who were sent away had to leave the people they loved most and live among strangers, sometimes for years. Life could be very hard for children who did not get on with their foster-parents, or who were often moved from one place to another.

Returning home could also be difficult. Children hardly knew their parents, and many were sad to leave their foster-homes. They often came back to families that had changed, with new step-parents, or younger brothers and sisters they had never met before. Settling down could be very difficult indeed.

There are even greater problems when children are taken away their homes for ever. One of the best known times when this happened was in 1975. The Americans were pulling out of Vietnam, after a bitter war. They were convinced that large numbers of children were in danger of being killed by the communist government that was set to take over, although the communists said they

Below During World War II, many children were sent out of the cities. There was a law to say that they had to be evacuated if they were suffering from life amid constant bombings and life in air-raid shelters. These under-fives were looked after at a residential school run by London's local government. They were well cared for by specially trained staff, but it is not easy for such young children to be away from home.

Above Older children left London for 'billets' in villages and country towns. Crowds of children gathered on railway stations and were sent many miles away from home. Each carried his or her gas mask which was meant to protect them if the Nazis dropped poisoned gas on the countryside. They also carried a little luggage – sometimes in boxes, or paper bags. The children all had labels on their collars with their names, their home address and the address they were going to.

had no intention of hurting the children.

Many of these children were the sons and daughters of Vietnamese women and American soldiers. Plane-loads of 'orphans' were taken out of Vietnam in what was known as a 'babylift'. The plan was to find them new, adoptive parents in the United States and other countries. Many ended up in orphanages. This was especially sad, since very often the children were not orphans at all, and did have families who wanted to care for them. They had simply lost touch with them.

Right Parting is always painful and separating a child from its mother may leave life-long psychological scars, although it may seem like the best thing to do at the time. This picture was taken in Greece in 1948, when a civil war was being fought for control of the country. The boy and his mother came from a mountainous area on the borders of Yugoslavia. At the time, two hundred thousand children were refugees. Many were taken to a safer area in the south of the country, near the city of Athens.

Shell-shocked

Like everyone else, children have to live through fear and horror in wartime. They may watch soldiers tear their homes apart and take their neighbours away as prisoners. They may watch friends and relatives, even their parents, die. They will spend much of their lives in a state of fear and anxiety as they listen to the gunfire and explosions around them.

Not surprisingly, children who have to live with this have all sorts of problems. Some cry constantly, or suffer nightmares and even hallucinations – seeing frightening things that are not really there. They may be permanently anxious, perhaps developing rashes, asthma and problems such as bed-wetting. Some children become lethargic and slow; there are even stories of children too frightened to get out of bed.

Coming to terms with the horror of war is difficult for everyone, especially children. But it is not always impossible. The children of Uganda have been especially hard-hit by civil war. There are many cases of them watching whole villages being massacred. When they reached the safety of orphanages, they were very disturbed and had terrifying nightmares, when they dreamed of the dreadful things they had seen. But these eventually stopped and, instead, they began to dream of their dead parents telling them to carry on with life. These children went on to try to help others in need.

Other children seem to find comfort in acting out the events they have watched. Workers in Palestinian refugee camps have watched children play at 'air raids' and rescue work afterwards.

Left This little boy in Northern Ireland has grown used to seeing soldiers and their tanks, and to hearing the sound of shooting. He may survive this without seeming to have many problems. But there is a serious chance that he will be very disturbed and frightened. Alternatively, he may decide to follow the tradition of street fighting and violence he has grown up with. Even while he is quite small, he may be out on the streets throwing stones at soldiers.

Obviously, children who live with war are much more anxious and afraid than those who do not. But even children who have not been involved in war may be very disturbed by the idea of it. This is especially true of nuclear war, which even young children know could destroy the whole world.

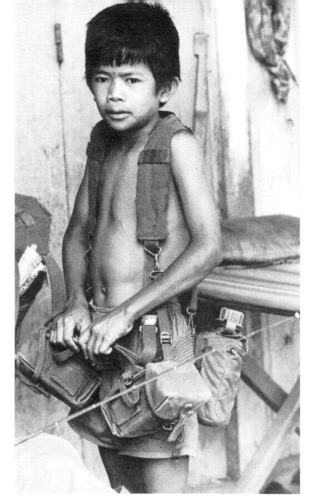

Right The taut features of this young Kampuchean boy reveal the stress and unhappiness in a young child forced to grow up quickly and cruelly into a harsh adult world. Kampuchea's Khmer Rouge government used children to help them stamp out opposition. Young children are often fiercely loyal and quite ruthless – perhaps unable to understand the consequences of their actions. The Khmer Rouge knew this and employed children as informers, encouraging them to tell the authorities about anyone – even their parents – who might not support them. Children were often put in charge of adults and were even able to order their executions. Having this sort of power at such a young age can leave children badly disturbed and damaged.

Below One of the worst things that can happen to any child is to lose a parent. In wartime, this is all too likely. This picture was taken in Poland in World War II. The girl had little chance to mourn her mother – she was probably too busy trying to survive herself. We need time to mourn when we lose someone we love. Without this, the girl would have suffered deeply for the rest of her life.

Physical injuries

Wars are about wounding and killing, and this is not confined to adult soldiers. Modern wars are fought among people's homes: in cities and in the countryside among farms and villages. Soldiers ransack homes in search of their enemies. Bombs fall on houses, rockets tear apart schools and hospitals, and fires rage through the streets. No one is safe from injury, least of all children.

War can leave everyone short of shelter, food and medicine. This is particularly damaging to young children, who lack the resistance to disease that healthy adults have. They do not have the strength to survive when there is not enough to eat, or when they are wounded, losing blood or are badly burned.

Children have special problems whenever they find themselves caught up in fighting. They may not be able to run fast enough to escape from gunfire, and they have few means of defending themselves.

These dangers are not confined to full-scale war. Street fighting and riots in Northern Ireland, for example, have led soldiers to use plastic or rubber bullets to break up a hostile crowd. In other countries, water cannons or even birdshot (designed for hunting birds) are used for the same reasons. Weapons of this sort can injure an adult badly, but have often proved fatal when used against children.

Physical injuries to adults also affect their children. Children whose parents are injured will grow up with an extra responsibility: to look after their parents as well as themselves – and possibly younger brothers and sisters as well.

Below Few people have suffered as much as the Kampucheans. These children are some of the half million or more refugees who left their homeland in the 1970s – first to escape the American bombing during the Vietnam war, and then to flee the murderous soldiers of Pol Pot's Khmer Rouge regime. Trying to survive in a refugee camp with little food and water is hard enough when you are strong and healthy. These young refugees on crutches have to contend with trying to start a new life with an arm or leg missing. This is especially hard for children who had once hoped to have a happy and active life.

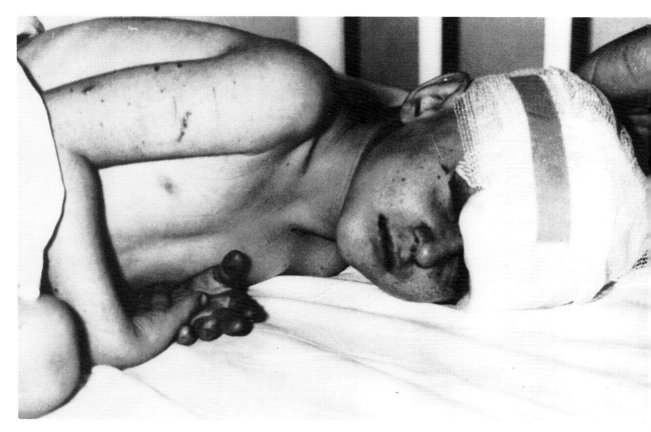

Above A child with a burned face lies in refugee camp hospital in Lebanon. Injury by burning is all too common in wartime. Either bombs set fire to buildings or cars, or electricity cables and gas mains hit by bombs cause explosions and fires. If there are no proper facilities for skin grafting – because the country is too poor or hospitals have been bombed – children like this boy may have to live with terrible scars for the rest of their lives – if, that is, they live at all.

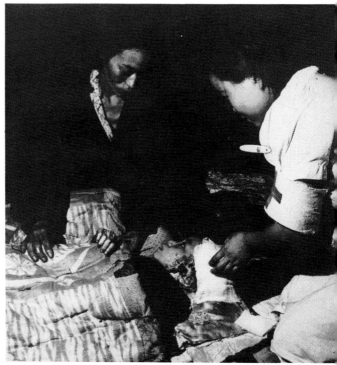

Right This child is suffering from terrible radiation burns, after American nuclear bombs were dropped on the Japanese cities of Hiroshima and Nagasaki in 1945. Even today, no one knows how many thousands died. In some places, all that was left of people were shadows on the walls and pavement. Everything else was burned away. One child described seeing 'people with burned flesh hanging off them like rags'. Other people were cut to pieces by flying glass and crushed by falling buildings. Afterwards, thousands died or became very sick as a result of radiation, which caused bleeding, diarrhoea and nausea. Children under the age of 10 developed different kinds of cancers and unborn children died in the womb or were malformed at birth.

(Quotation from *Children of Hiroshima*, © Publishing Committee for *Children of Hiroshima*, 1980.)

The means to survive

Wars cost vast sums of money. Each minute, the richer countries of the world spend over $1.5 million on arms. In the same minute, in poorer countries, thirty children die for want of food or inexpensive medicines. A single nuclear submarine costs as much as the whole education budget for more than twenty developing countries with more than 160 million schoolchildren.

We could ask, would this money be spent on poor countries, if it was not being spent on war? Of course, there is no way of knowing. What we *can* see, is how much the poor countries themselves spend on weapons, and how this leads to suffering and even death among ordinary people who are not themselves caught up in the fighting.

Above These children are in a refugee camp in Jordan. Living in a war-torn community often means going without basic facilities. Water must be carried from wells and standpipes into homes. There is no proper drainage, so dirty water, flowing in the streets, may infect the drinking water supply. Disease spreads and the young are specially at risk.

Countries that have almost no money to spare still buy weapons, aircraft, tanks and all sorts of other equipment in order to fight wars. This is not usually because they actually want to fight. It is more likely that they feel threatened by other countries, or by rebels within their own country.

In Mozambique, for example, the government has to spend huge sums of money fighting rebels who are backed by a much richer country – South Africa. Because of this war, the government of Mozambique has not been able to build up the schools, hospitals and all the other things they had planned to do when the country became independent.

Throughout the world, huge sums of money are spent on armies and weapons, while ordinary people are in desperate need. Things are made worse by the effects of war, as armies and their weapons may actually destroy existing towns and villages.

Above Children scrabble through a slag heap in search of a few pieces of coal. After the end of World War II, the city of Berlin was cut off from the outside world as the superpowers argued over the right to control it. Five years of fighting had left the city in ruins, with little food and no fuel. People were afraid of the winter and the cold and hunger it would bring.

Right With his parents dead or missing, this young Ugandan child was lucky to have his older brother to help and care for him. He was just one of millions of victims of a bitter civil war in the 1980s. Food was scarce and large numbers of children suffered from starvation and disease. With its economy in ruins, the government could provide little health care. The children's wing of the country's main hospital depended on charities such as the Save the Children Fund to provide medical care.

Ruins and rubble

Modern warfare causes destruction on a huge scale. With the development of heavy artillery and bomber aircraft, no civilian town or village is safe from attack.

In World War II the Germans invented a new kind of warfare called *Blitzkrieg*, or lightning war. From September 1940 to May 1941, German planes dive-bombed London nearly every night. It was called The Blitz. Huge areas of the city were destroyed. During the War, bombing, artillery fire and street fighting devastated such major cities as Berlin, Budapest, Dresden, Coventry, Leningrad, Milan and Rotterdam. Fire bombs destroyed the heart of Tokyo and most of Yokohama.

Not only houses are destroyed by bombing. Schools, hospitals, roads, trains and vital services like electricity and water, suddenly do not exist. In Vietnam, chemicals were sprayed from aircraft to strip the trees of all vegetation so that the enemy could be seen more easily. Crops were destroyed, and farmers' livelihoods with them.

Above, right In World War I newly developed weapons such as tanks, heavy artillery and bomber aircraft caused more damage to buildings than in any previous wars. Bombing and shelling destroyed the industrial and community lives of many European towns and villages, closed or destroyed schools, factories, roads and railways. In Eastern Europe and the Balkans, millions of people fled their homes, terrified by the threat of invasion. They sought shelter in the ruins of blasted buildings. After the war those who tried to return home often found their towns and villages no longer existed.

Below, right 'There wasn't anything left – our house, or the camellia tree, or the garden, or Mummy's sewing machine, or Daddy's books, or my picture books or the kitchen where my Mummy used to make tempura, or the swing Brother and I used to swing on, or the telephone or anything.'
Kayano Nagai was four years old when the atomic bomb was dropped on Hiroshima in Japan, reducing everything to rubble for miles around. Young children need the security of familiar surroundings. The loss of them, in addition to the loss of friends and family can be devastating.

(Quotation from *We of Nagasaki*, by Takashi Nagai, Ace Books, 1958.)

At the end of World War II in August 1945, the Americans dropped two atomic bombs, one on Hiroshima, Japan, with a population of 300,000, the other on Nagasaki, population 250,000.

First there was a blinding flash, then a deafening bang, then the mushroom cloud, a pillar of flame with a deathly grey smoke umbrella. The cities burned for an entire day. Almost nothing was left standing. Half their populations were killed. Nowadays we have nuclear weapons which are 1,000 times more powerful than these.

People whose communities have been destroyed are forced to take what few belongings they can carry and then start the long walk to find a place of refuge.

Above Civil war broke out in the Lebanon in 1975. Although the war officially ended in 1976 there has been trouble ever since. The capital, Beirut is a battleground, divided between rival factions. Houses have been bombed, rebuilt and bombed again. About half the families in central Beirut have at one time or another been forced to live in their cellars or to leave their homes. Children have no proper education because their schools have been bombed time and time again. Their playground is a mass of rubble and dangerous twisted metal spikes. One mother and her two small children fled to the countryside where, for several weeks, they lived in a shack in a field and the children ate grass.

The long walk

When a war breaks out – especially a civil war – fighting drives people from their homes. Refugees are a by-product of almost every war.

People become refugees for a variety of reasons. Some are individuals who have opposed their government. They are afraid of being arrested or even killed.

Many run away from their homes because they are in danger of being caught up in the shooting or bombing. Sometimes they live in areas where guerrilla armies have their bases. Government troops suspect the people of hiding their enemies. They attack communities, murdering people and wrecking homes. Survivors flee, afraid of being killed outright or of starving after their crops and livestock have been destroyed.

When people leave their homes as refugees, they can take very few possessions with them. They carry what they can, and set out to find somewhere they think will be safer.

Left These people are refugees from an area of Ethiopia called Tigray. A civil war, along with years of drought, have worked together to drive people from their homes. Carrying almost nothing, they make their way to refugee camps where they hope that they will get enough food to survive. In recent years, international charities have been trying to help the Tigrayan people. They hope to rebuild their farms, so that they can return home and live there in safety.

Right Between 1936 and 1939, there was a bitter civil war in Spain. Supporters of an elected, left-wing government were eventually defeated by the right-wing 'nationalists'. In January 1939, thousands of people, afraid for their lives, fled across the Pyrenees into France. By February 1939, more than 170,000 women and children had made their way into France, along with 10,000 wounded soldiers. Thousands more were to follow. Onlookers described how children arrived clutching broken toys – all that was left of their former life.

Such journeys are often long and dangerous. An individual on the run may have to use a false name and travel in secret. He or she may have to hide for days or even weeks before they can reach another country where they will be safe.

Wars bring extra problems to people whose lives are difficult anyway. In areas of the world such as Ethiopia, where drought and poor soil make farming difficult, conflict makes matters worse. Once war breaks out, there is little chance of help being brought to isolated communities. Governments may not want to aid people they think are supporting their enemies.

As a result, people find themselves in danger of starving. This forces them to leave their homes, often in very large numbers. They travel in groups of thousands, on foot, across mountains or deserts. They may already be weak from shortage of food and water, and perhaps sick as well. Many die on their way to what they think will be safety.

Right Only half the population of Kampuchea lived through the time when their country was ruled by the Khmer Rouge. These refugees have left a country where there was almost no food and where hospitals, clinics and schools had been deliberately destroyed. When they eventually reached the camps, they were often sick and exhausted. These people, in a camp in Thailand, lie exhausted, with their baby in a cardboard box – along with their tiny amount of food. What sort of life can this little girl expect? Years of wandering from camp to camp – or a grudging acceptance in a foreign land?

Passing through

There are refugees all over the world. Some manage to settle in new countries, far from home. If they are lucky, they find jobs and homes where they can settle down safely until they are free to go home.

But for most refugees, the end of their long journey is nothing more than a makeshift camp – a group of tents or huts with little food, poor water supplies and almost nothing else. Settlements like these are not designed to be permanent communities. People may try to grow vegetables or even keep animals, but all too often they have to rely on outside organizations for help. Many refugee camps – like those in Sudan, for example – are in countries which are too poor to be able to do much even for their own people. Refugees can expect nothing from them. Instead they must depend on United Nations organizations and aid groups to provide food and the other things they need to stay alive.

Few people plan to remain in these camps but, sadly, they often find that their stay there is not as temporary as they had hoped. War, famine and political unrest mean that

Above More than two and a half million Afghani people have taken refuge in Pakistan. They have left their homes in order to get away from the civil war being fought against the Soviet backed government. These children's fathers may be involved in that bitter war – if they are still alive. Camps are often densely populated. The sewage system is usually an open drain flowing between the dwellings, where the children play. There is seldom enough food, schooling or medical care. Young children grow up knowing no home other than the camp.

people have to live as refugees for years on end. In the Middle East, there are camps that have existed for forty years. Whole generations have grown up in them.

Sometimes groups of people flee to another country as refugees, but end up settling there for ever. In the modern world, governments try to make this difficult, but things were different in the past. All through the last century, for example, Jewish refugees arrived in Britain from Central Europe. Others went to the United States, where vast numbers of people from all over Europe were also settling. The people who began as refugees became citizens of a new country.

Above These are 'boat people' – Vietnamese refugees living in uncomfortable conditions in a camp in Hong Kong. Since the communist government took over Vietnam, many refugees have left the country. They set sail in leaky boats across the south China sea – hoping to be rescued by passing ships or to eventually reach safety and the chance of a new, permanent home. Many never reach the end of their journey. There is no way of finding out just how many have been shipwrecked and drowned, or attacked and murdered by pirates.

Right This little boy has reached the end of a long journey. Now he is settling in a new country, and is learning a new language and way of life. The boat people do not expect to go home to Vietnam – at least not very soon. But neither do they want to stay for long in the crowded, unhealthy conditions of the refugee camps in Hong Kong. They hope that, like this child and his family, they will be accepted as immigrants into some other country – perhaps the United States or Canada.

A helping hand

Wars leave a trail of death and destruction behind them. Afterwards, the people are left with the huge task of building new homes, hospitals and factories. Few governments can afford this. Most need help from outside – from friendly governments, United Nations agencies and a range of different charities that work for the poor.

Today, we often think of aid as being something the poorest countries need. But it is not so long since much of Europe was also desperately poor. World War II left many countries devastated, without food and without any money to rebuild basic services. Large numbers of children were homeless and starving, while the industries and farms that could have made money had been destroyed. American aid was poured into western Europe in order to rebuild the shattered economies.

Since that time there have been many more countries in need, many more starving children and wrecked schools and hospitals all over the world. But giving and accepting help is not always a simple matter. Foreign governments may offer aid in order to try to influence events in the country they are helping. When one government accepts help from another, it must be very careful indeed.

Sometimes foreign governments actually refuse to help a country because they do not approve of the way it is being run. They may do this even when it is desperately poor. For example, when the Vietnamese invaded Kampuchea (also known as Cambodia) in 1979, they found the Khmer Rouge government had destroyed almost everything. But many Western governments refused to help the Vietnamese rebuild Kampuchea because they disapproved of the invasion. The Kampucheans had to depend on charities, such as Oxfam, for the help they so badly needed.

Below The best way to help with rebuilding a country is to help the people do it themselves. In Uganda, many people were short of food because of a long civil war. Children became sick because they had not had enough of the right food to eat. These women are learning how to help their children get a proper diet and become strong and healthy again.

Above Four-year-old Elefteria Tranopoulos was the only child left in the Greek village of Oxia at the end of World War II. She kisses her new leather shoes, a gift from the United Nations Childrens Emergency Fund (UNICEF). The Fund was created in 1946 to mount relief programmes for the children of war-torn Europe. It provided food, clothing and medical care. It has now given aid to millions of children throughout the world. Its aim is to give help to children 'without discrimination because of race, creed, nationality, status or political belief'. For this reason UNICEF cared for mothers and children on both sides of the Vietnam conflict, and both sides in the Nigerian civil war.

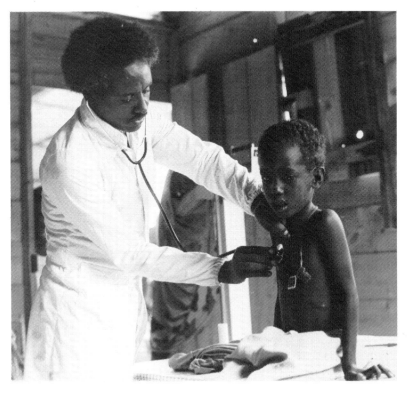

Left One of the smallest casualties of war receives medical treatment at a camp for Ethiopian refugees. The long journey to a refugee camp may only be the beginning of a child's problems. Camps are often dirty and overcrowded, with little to eat and no clean water. There is usually little money around to improve things. The refugees very often depend on aid from abroad for basic medical services and even the food they need to survive.

Hope for the future

It's very easy to think that wars are inevitable. Certainly, if we look around the world today, it's hard not to believe it. Not only are there bitter wars happening on every continent, but it seems that we all accept war as a part of our lives. We make toy weapons. We watch films about war and violence. All in all, it seems sometimes that we actually like war.

But perhaps all this could change – if we wanted it to. Many people believe that we should not continue to show war as an exciting adventure. They think it is wrong to give toy weapons to little boys, and to teach children that it is always right and proper to fight for their country and its government.

Most of all, they believe that we should not have weapons with which to attack others. They are especially worried about the huge numbers of nuclear weapons held by the United States, the Soviet Union and even smaller countries like Britain as well. They believe that these should all be destroyed, and welcome proposals to get rid of them.

It all sounds like a good idea – but it isn't always that simple. Every war that ever happens has a long history behind it. There will always be people who feel passionately that they have a cause for which they must fight. They see war as a 'necessary evil', which has to be undertaken in order to end up with a better situation in the long run.

Left This U.S. soldier in Vietnam was probably told in his training that he would be 'taking objectives' (meaning attacking enemy strongholds) and that he was fighting people who were evil and dangerous What his training was unlikely to have prepared him for was dealing with the personal, human suffering that war brings. He may be a father himself and yet he is taught to deprive innocent children – like his own – of their mothers and fathers, all in the name of 'peace'.

Whether or not you agree with this depends on what you think of the reasons for the conflict.

What is clear is that wars are terrible experiences to live through. It is also clear that they are started, and continued, by adults. Children are caught up in something which they cannot control, and are bound to suffer. Even those children who actually take up arms themselves are in a sense victims of war.

Left Children are the world's future – but what sort of future is this? This boy is in Belfast, and he has already taken to wearing the clothes and manner of a guerrilla fighter. He certainly believes he has right on his side – and this is what he has been taught throughout his life. But has he ever had a chance to enjoy just being a child?

Below Nuclear weapons exist in many countries of the world. There enough to destroy the world several times over. Many children fear that nuclear war will end the world before they grow up. Some join protests to try to convince the government to give a lead by getting rid of Britain's own nuclear weapons. Children have taken part in the peace movement in other ways too. Some write to the world leaders, asking them to give up their weapons.

Reference

Fact file

Afghanistan lies north of India. It is ruled by a pro-Russian government with the help of Soviet troops, who invaded the country in 1979. Rebels aiming to overthrow this government have been fighting since that time. Large numbers of people, including many children, fled to neighbouring Pakistan, where they live as refugees.

Aid agencies are bodies such as OXFAM, the Save the Children Fund, War on Want, Christian Aid, the Catholic Fund for Overseas Development (CAFOD) and so on. These contribute money and help to countries that need it. Aid agencies such as these are independent of governments.

The **Crimean War** of 1854–56 involved Britain, France and Sardinia. They declared war on Russia because she invaded the Balkans and sank the Turkish fleet.

The **Crusades** were a series of wars fought between 1095 and 1271. Soldiers from Europe went out to the Middle East to fight Muslims for control of the country we now call Israel.

El Salvador is in Central America. It has been ruled for many years by a right-wing regime and, since 1979 has had a U.S.-backed military government. People began protesting in the late 1970s, aiming for more land and jobs for the poor. By 1980, there was full-scale civil war, with left-wing guerrillas on one side and government troops on the other. Unofficial 'death squads' killed people who opposed the government. The troops bombed areas of El Salvador and neighbouring Honduras in an attempt to destroy guerrilla strongholds. As a result, thousands of refugees have been driven from their homes in the war-torn areas and have sought shelter in Honduras.

The **Holocaust** is the name usually given to the murder of 6,000,000 Jewish people by the Nazis during World War II.

Ireland is divided into two parts: the independent Republic of Ireland in the south, and British-ruled Northern Ireland. Most of the large minority of Catholic northerners would prefer Ireland to be entirely independent. A few have taken up arms as members of the Provisional Irish Republican Army (I.R.A.), in order to fight for this. Protestant illegal armies have also formed, and are devoted to fighting Catholics and the I.R.A.

Kampuchea, also sometimes called Cambodia, has suffered war since 1970. After being bombed by the Americans during the Vietnam War, it was taken over by the radical Khmer Rouge in 1975.

They were responsible for killing more than a million people, including children, and many more died of starvation and disease. A Vietnamese invasion in 1979 ended this regime, but civil war continues. Millions of Kampucheans have left home and become refugees.

Kurdestan is a region of Asia. It lies across areas of Turkey, Syria, Iran and Iraq. Since the 1920s, the Kurdish people have campaigned and fought for self-government. The countries who rule Kurdestan have refused to allow this and have put down rebellions among the Kurds. The people have suffered at the hands of several governments, especially that of Iraq. Kurdestan is virtually in a state of civil war.

Lebanon is a country in the Middle East, bordering on Israel. Throughout the 1980s, it has been the centre of a civil war between various warring groups of Lebanese. These include people belonging to the Christian religion and various groups of Muslims. In addition, Lebanon is home for thousands of Palestinian refugees from Israel. These people have been attacked several times by both Lebanese groups and Israeli troops.

Mozambique is in southern Africa, bordering on, among other countries, South Africa and Zimbabwe. It was colonized by Portugal for many years and has been independent since 1975, following a long war of liberation. The present government of Mozambique has been forced to spend a great deal of effort and money fighting 'rebels', funded and supported by the government of South Africa.

Palestine is the name once given to the country now called Israel. Large numbers of Arab people who once lived there fled when Israel was formed in 1948. Many still live, with their children and grandchildren, in refugee camps in neighbouring Jordan and Lebanon.

The **Spanish civil war** took place between 1936 and 1939. A left-wing government was elected, but was defeated by right-wing forces and a military government under General Franco eventually won power. Spain was ruled by the military until the death of Franco in 1975. He was followed by new rulers who planned to return Spain to democratic government, and elections were held in 1977. In 1982, the Spanish people voted in their first socialist government since 1939.

Uganda is a country in East Africa. It gained independence from Britain in 1962. For many years Uganda was ruled by dictators who were responsible for large numbers of deaths. In 1980, a civil war broke out against the then president,

Milton Obote. The rebels – called the National Resistance Movement – soon found they had many children in their ranks. These were orphans whose parents were killed by government troops. The NRM took power in 1986 and now rules Uganda. Many of the children are now in special army schools.

UNICEF is the United Nations Children's Emergency Fund. It was formed in 1948 in order to help children who were suffering as a result of World War II. It is still working in war-torn areas of the world.

World War I was fought between 1914 and 1918. It was fought mainly in Europe, with forces from Britain and its colonies, along with troops from other European countries, fighting Germany. About 14,000,000 people – soldiers and civilians – died in this war. People hoped it would be 'the war to end wars'.

World War II was fought between 1939 and 1945. Germany, led by Adolf Hitler and his Nazi party, had invaded much of Europe. Japan joined the war in 1941, by attacking the American naval base at Pearl Harbour in Hawaii. The United States then fought back and joined forces with British troops (along with troops from the Commonwealth) and those of the Soviet Union. This war was even more devastating than World War I. An estimated 55,000,000 military and civilians died.

International law

International law gives special protection to children. This came about after World War II and is set out in the Fourth Geneva Convention. At first, children were covered by the law as civilians – that is, people not fighting.

In 1977, certain additions to the laws, called Protocols were added. These are especially relevant to children. Some of the rules they set out can be summarized in this way:
1. Children should be 'the object of special respect' and not subjected to any indecent assault.
2. Children should get special care when they are caught up in an armed conflict.
3. Children should be evacuated from areas of armed conflict.
4. Children should be given priority, along with expectant mothers, in the distribution of aid.
5. Families should be reunited when they have been split up by war.
6. Orphans should be able to continue their education and religion.
7. Children arrested in wartime should be kept separately from adults.

8. The death penalty should not be inflicted on anyone under the age of 18.
9. Children aged 15 and under should not be recruited into the armed forces.

These are just a few of the rules to protect children. Not all countries have signed them – and reality is almost always a long way from the ideals set out here.

Further reading

ADULT REFERENCE

Children and War: proceedings of a symposium at Siutio Baths, Finland, GIPRI, IPB, Peace Union of Finland 1983.

Children in Conflict, Morris Fraser, Penguin, Harmondsworth, 1974.

Children of War, Roger Rosenblatt, Anchor Press/ Doubleday, New York, 1983.

The Smallest Pawns in the Game, Peter Townsend, Granada, London 1980.

None But Ourselves: Masses vs media in the making of Zimbabwe, by Julie Frederikse, with photographs by Biddy Partridge, Heinemann, London, 1983.

Children of Hiroshima, The Publishing Committee for 'Children of Hiroshima', Tokyo 1980.

Unforgettable Fire: Pictures drawn by Atomic Bomb survivors, edited by Japan Broadcasting Corporation, Wildwood House, London 1977.'

The Hiroshima Story, by Toshi Maruki, Adam and Charles Black, London 1980.

BOOKS FOR CHILDREN

People Then and Now: A divided people in Ireland, by Brian Haigh, Macdonald, London 1986.

Flashpoints: The Vietnam War, by Richard Edwards, Wayland, Hove 1986.

Afghanistan (A first book), by Henry Gilford, Franklin Watts, London, 1980.

Wartime Children 1939–1945, by Elearnor Allen, A and C Black, London 1975.

We of Nagasaki, by Takashi Nagai, Ace Books, 1958.

Index